12 Healing Steps
Out of the Pain of Abuse

The Survivor Diaries

Comfort Food Recipes

A Three-Part Series

We are all broken and wounded

in this world. Some choose to grow strong

at the broken places.

-- Harold J. Duarte-Bernhardt

12 Healing Steps
Out of the Pain of Abuse

The Survivor Diaries

Comfort Food Recipes

A Three-Part Series

Barbara E. Kompik
Editor: Leta Ann Luurtsema

"…offering hope and healing to those
Who have been abused."

CreateSpace.com, an Amazon Company

12 Healing Steps Out of the Pain of Abuse
The Survivor Diaries
Comfort Food Recipes
Copyright 2013 by Barbara E. Kompik

Requests for information should be addressed to:
barbarakompik@hotmail.com

Visit her website for more information on abuse:
www.HealingfromAbuse.webs.com

Any Internet addresses (websites, blogs, etc.) and
telephone numbers in this book are offered as a resource.
They are not intended in any way to be or imply an
endorsement by CreateSpace.com, nor does
CreateSpace.com vouch for the content of these sites and
numbers for the life of this book.

Editor: Leta Ann Luurtsema,
leta.editing@gmail.com
Photographer: Hannah Kostal

This book is dedicated to my husband and children who kept me alive through my deepest depression. You are the loves of my life and I couldn't have healed if it weren't for you. You each are incredible beyond description. For my husband Dale and our three children, Tasha, Natalie, Dale II, and Will, my son-in-law, many thanks.

Thank you, Tasha, for your comfort, sensitivity and humor as I struggled through the pain. To Natalie, thanks for your comforting words and your listening ear on many occasions on the phone. To Dale II, my strength and strong arm, who kept us intact through the chaos. To Will, thank you for loving my daughter and comforting her during the toughest times. I adore you all.

To Dale, the love of my life, whose perseverance went far beyond the call of duty. Thank you for always being there. I love you forever.

Contributors who helped shape this book are Leta Ann Luurtsema, my editor and Eva Kostal. Eva, thanks for your blessings each day and the wisdom you shared in the writing of this book. You are helping to touch many lives for the Lord.

"This is my path through the darkness and the woods, and although I may not have chosen it willingly, it is mine, and the broken glass from the damage sparkles like diamonds."

Doni Goodman, survivor

Preface

I grew up in a very strict home, and since I didn't agree with all of the rules, I was considered a troublemaker in my family. We were to adhere to all the rules: keep family secrets, obey the authoritarian (dad) without question, do what they said, not what they did, and go to church every Sunday. No one had opinions of his or her own. There was no love or nurturing. We were left to grow up on our own.

I was the different one; the one that always made waves. I rocked the boat by thinking differently than my folks. I couldn't wait to get out of the house. I felt worthless, unloved, and alone.

I was told by my mother in the strictest voice, pointing her finger in my face, growling, "You are NOT an individual! You are part of the family!" This went along with their totalitarian ways. I was excommunicated from the family emotionally. I had terrible self-esteem and many times I just wanted to die because it hurt so badly.

Because I was so different from my family, my parents would cry out in desperation, "What's wrong with you?! Do we need to take you to a psychiatrist?!" Dad's voice boomed down to my heart and settled in the depths of my soul. Hearing those words made me panic at the thought of being locked up in a psychiatric ward somewhere, and never being heard from again. I knew they would never love me like I needed to be loved.

All of this led to leading a terrible life of rebellion and pain. I went against everything my parents taught me and led a hard life.

When I married, my husband and I had trouble and argued all of the time. We began to see a zillion counselors and no one could help us. They all said my problems were caused by PMS. When my husband and I argued, I didn't remember most of what I said and argued vehemently that I didn't say them. It was so maddening, until he bought a book called <u>Secret Survivors of Incest.</u> I wouldn't have anything to do with the book and it scared me even to look at it. He read it instead, and started asking me questions to which I could say 'yes, that fit my life.' Through the book, and recalling ordinary memories, we learned that I was a survivor of incest by the hands of family members when I was very small. I learned this when I was 45 years old.

Incest leaves terrible marks. Of the 35 symptoms listed in the book, I had 34, and one of those was dissociation. I learned that I had more than a dozen parts, all with names and certain roles that they played. I also learned that I could talk to them and help them understand the trauma they'd been through. I found a wonderful therapist who believed me and knew how to deal with it. I knew a miracle had happened.

I was in therapy for three years before I was diagnosed with Bipolar Personality Disorder, which is characterized by extreme high and low mood swings, Borderline Personality Disorder, which is black and white thinking, and Dissociation, the splitting off of different personalities within one's internal core. It was very scary at first to think I had this disorder, but the more I learned about it, I felt I was very blessed to have survived the trauma in that way, instead of possibly losing my mind entirely, or losing my life through suicide. I was able to get to know myself intimately. On rare occasions, my dissociation comes back to remind me of where I've come from. But I feel that I have been healed of the trauma and chaos it presented in my life.

I was suicidal at times, because the pain was so great I didn't think I could endure it. I would get so hopeless and desperate, I'd cry, praying that God would take my pain away. I'd cry, 'I DON'T WANT TO LIVE ANYMORE! I JUST WANT TO DIE! HELP ME, LORD!" He would be there, reminding me of my own darling children to keep me alive and that my life meant something to those I loved. My loved ones literally saved my life.

It took seven years to heal emotionally enough to be out of therapy and on medications only. That was a huge accomplishment for me. I also healed to the point that my relationship with my abusers is one of love, acceptance, and forgiveness. I couldn't have done that on my own.

I'm in college now, studying for a Social Work degree, and I have high goals I know I can achieve that I never dreamed I could when I was ill. Even though it was very difficult; beyond my capacity, I thank God that I've gone through it so that I can better understand and help others.

I now have a website called "Healing from Abuse" where I share my story and encourage others to share theirs in order to heal. It also has my original site on MySpace and the conversations that the members and I have had and the issues that each person was dealing with. There are many people who have visited, and many countries around the world are represented on that site.

Now I can share what broke my life into a million charred pieces and took me on a most painful path. I can tell others that there is hope and healing to those who have been abused.

God can take a broken heart and heal it completely, where there is no more pain.

Love and Blessings as you read this book, Barbara

Contents

Part I

12 Healing Steps
Out of the Pain of Abuse

Part II

The Survivor Diaries

Part III

Comfort Food Recipes

Additional Information

"Every experience God gives us, every person He puts into our lives, is the perfect preparation for the future only He can see."

~ Corrie ten Boom

Your Healing Journal

This is your safe place to write your memories, thoughts, and

dreams as you travel on your healing journey. Journaling should

be done on a daily basis, in order to promote healing. One thing

you can be assured: healing comes slowly, but it does come ...

and it will meet you in a new place.

Don't confuse your path with your destination. Just because it's stormy now doesn't mean that you aren't headed for sunshine.

~Unknown

Step One

Make the Choice

Making the choice to heal takes a lot of courage. It means that you must be willing to take a look at yourself and see where you need to do some adjusting in order to feel better. It is admitting some difficult things that may be hard to face … and that is why we are.

You cannot do this alone. You need someone beside you, cheering you on, encouraging you, supporting you, validating you, and helping you to see the truth. It takes a conscious effort to heal. It takes perseverance. It takes work. It doesn't just happen to you – you have to step out and up to the plate and declare, "I am going to heal no matter what it takes because I deserve a life that is without all of this unbearable

pain! "So as you begin this journey toward wholeness and

healing, I will ask you to interact here and declare your

willingness to commit to your own healing.

If you have made the choice to take control of your life

and make a difference for yourself.

My Commitment to Healing

I am committed to healing. I will do what it takes to

make my life better for myself. I will decide for myself what is

good for me and what is not. I will choose only the good things

for my life and reject the bad. I will have to make some hard choices, but I know that in the end, it will be worth it for me. I

do not want to live like this any longer. I want help. I want

healing. I am committed to my healing, every day for the rest of

my life. I understand that it will not happen overnight, but it

will take a lot of work on my part to listen to myself, to get to

know myself and to trust something or someone other than

myself for the good of me, because I do not have or know all the

answers.

I am committed to listening and doing what is required

to bring peace and wholeness for myself. I will commit to not

harming myself in any way any longer.

I will heal! I will overcome, because I am worth every

minute of it!

You have just made the most difficult decisions you will ever

have to make on your journey to healing!

Love and blessings,

~Barbara

I have learned now, that while those who speak about Ones' miseries
usually hurt,

Those who keep silence hurt more.

- C.S. Lewis

Step Two

Tell the Secret, Share the Story

A's someone who has been abused, it has been engrained into our souls that we are not to tell, no matter what. So we lock everything inside and throw away the key. The trouble with that is, it was defiled garbage that was dumped on us, and you know what happens to that stuff when it is locked up in a warm, moist place, don't you? It begins to REALLY stink!

That's what is happening to you. The crap that you put up with all of your life, or the traumatic moments that you experienced in rape, incest, or molestation; whatever abuse you have endured, has all been manure that has been heaped upon you, a shovelful at a time, a bushel at a time, or truckload at a time, and now you are suffering from the smell and nauseating existence of it in your life.

You need to get that out of your system. The only way to do that is to tell the secrets and share your story. It is the only way. You need to tell someone, anyone who will listen to you and take you seriously, hear you, validate you, support you, and understand you, without criticism or judgment. You cannot do this alone. You need someone there, helping you scoop out the manure so you can breathe again. There really IS fresh air out there, and it's time for you to begin breathing it, for it is yours for the taking.

Begin to release the memories within, by telling your

story in a spiral notebook or journal. It's a safe place to journal

all of your memories, emotions, and feelings, all of the

experiences that are hard to face alone. Keep it in a safe place.

You can say anything you need to say and you will not be

punished for it. On the contrary! You will be understood and

applauded that you have had the courage to let your secrets out.

It takes strength and a lot of guts, but it needs to be done.

It's just like the surgeon who needs to cut into you to

remove shrapnel deep within the tissues of your body. You've

been on the frontlines and have been shot. You have been in a

war zone and you have been wounded, over and over again,

filled with bullets of every shape and size. If those aren't

removed, then you will bleed to death, slowly but surely. It is

critical to get the stuff out of you that is causing the pain so that

you can be healed.

It doesn't mean that the memories won't be there

anymore. It doesn't mean that once you begin to share, that

"poof!" everything will disappear. No. I do not begin to claim

that. But the pain will begin to ooze out and you will feel

tremendous pressure released from you, and you will begin to

slowly make progress in your healing. Yes, you will remember,

but it won't be as painful anymore.

I know that you wish this hadn't happened to you. I'm

so sorry it did, but we can't change any of that. I know there is a

grieving process that you must go through, knowing the loss of

innocence, the loss of happiness, and the loss of everything you

ever dreamed of, but instead of destroying you, we are going to

make this bad thing turn around and create something

beautiful for you. It can happen for you. Believe me, it can

happen. But you must be willing to do what it takes to allow

that to happen. It won't be overnight, and it may take a long

time. But it is worth every painful step, because along the way

you will find beautiful things within yourself that you couldn't

see before.

So I encourage you, start your journal today. Name it

whatever you wish, but know that it is YOUR story. Then come

back to it each day and add more to it, little by little, whatever

you can remember at the time, whatever is happening to you

during the day, so that you will begin to see the progress that

you make along the way.

Your story needs to be shared ... for your own sake and

for the sake of others. You have been holding the secrets far too

long and they are destroying you. Let the secrets out.

Love and blessings,

~Barbara

My Commitment to
Telling My Story

I am committed to letting out the secrets within me that

are holding me captive to this pain. I want to tell my story. I am

committed to allowing my mind to recall what it needs to in

order to bring healing to my mind, body, and soul. I will journal

here and let those memories out in this safe place. I will share

what I feel. I need to share here in order to heal. No matter how

many details I need to include, no matter what emotions

surface, I will share them here. I am committed to adding

something each day, no matter how small, no matter how great, so that I can daily take care of myself and get this garbage out of

my system. I understand that I need to do this in order to

honor and take care of myself as I deserve to be cared for. I am

committed to telling the secrets and the story because of what

my abuser/s did to me, and did not want to be found out.

That's why they threatened me, told me I was worthless, and

every other negative thing they told me about myself, so that

they could squash me into believing that I didn't matter. But I

DO matter. I am a person. I think and feel. I hurt and cry.

What I think matters and it matters very much. No one can tell

me otherwise, because I believe that my life matters. Even if I

don't feel it right now, I will begin to let it soak into my being and begin to believe it ... because I have a lot to offer others and

they are just waiting for me to open myself up to them. My story

matters. It makes up a part of me, but it does not define me. I

have the control to define myself, no matter what that definition

may be, and no one can tell me that I don't matter anymore. I

will write my memories here, so that I can get rid of the pain

and start all over, rewriting my own life as I wish it to be. I have

that power. I have that control! I can do this, because I am

worth every minute of it!

Keep your face to the sunshine,

and you will not see the shadows.

~Helen Keller

Step Three

Acknowledge Your Emotions

Ok, here's another tough one. I keep saying these are difficult, don't I? One of the first

things that my therapist did with me was

to tell me to get comfortable in my chair and close my eyes.

Then I was to tell her what I felt.

I didn't have a clue as to what she was talking about! All I could

say was, "umm uh, I don't know!" It was difficult to focus on my

body and be aware of my bodily sensations and my emotions.

So she showed me how to do it. She settled into her chair, closed

her eyes, and began to breathe slowly. She was silent for a

moment, and then she began to speak slowly, softly,

methodically. And she said:

"I feel my legs on the chair. I feel my hands on my lap. I feel the skin on my arm from my hand touching it. I feel my feet on the floor. I feel the tenseness in my neck. I hear ringing in my left ear. I hear footsteps outside the door. I feel my breathing, my chest rising up and down. I feel warmth in my legs ..."

She continued like that for about one minute. Then she had me try. I closed my eyes and settled into my chair. It felt very strange to focus on something that I THOUGHT I had been aware of, but found that I was merely going through the motions of living, without knowing what it felt like to be inside my body.

When I listed what I was aware of, she asked me what I felt;

what emotion I was feeling. I didn't have any idea of that either.

I wasn't even sure what emotions there were besides love, hate,

and anger. I couldn't name any. As she prodded me on, I said

that I felt tense. Then she asked me where in my body I felt it.

This was hard to describe; hard to focus in on where that

emotion was letting itself be known.

Then I felt tightness in my chest. I felt tingling in my arms,

warmth that seemed to increase as I focused on it.

She talked to me softly as my eyes were closed, instructing me

through the whole exercise.

"What are you aware of in your body?"

"What emotions are you feeling?"

"Where do you feel those emotions?"

We practiced it for five minutes. Then she encouraged

me to go home and set the timer and sit quietly for just two

minutes and practice it, to become aware of my surroundings,

to become aware of my feelings, to become aware of what was

happening inside my body, to become aware of me, deep within

myself.

We are so prone to just react to our environment; not

really knowing or tuning in to what our bodies are telling us,

what messages our emotions want to give us. We just simply

'are' most of the time, without any thought to our emotions. So we miss out on so much that we have to give ourselves, because

it is in listening to ourselves, listening to our emotions and body

sensations, and acknowledging them and focusing in on them

that we give honor to ourselves and respect ourselves. And in

doing so, we take back the control of ourselves that we lost when

we were abused.

When we don't listen to our emotions and body

sensations, they start screaming to be heard. This comes out in

self-destructive ways ... cutting, suicidal thoughts, anger, over-

eating, breaking things, drugs, and alcohol, etc. They turn

against us because we aren't listening to them. And when they

are not released and allowed to be known, they create turmoil and havoc in our lives, which makes us feel out of control again

and chaotic.

So it is very simple. You need to simply name the

emotions that you are feeling as they come up, focus in on where

your body is feeling that emotion and just let it be. Focus on,

and listen to it, very quietly within. There are no judgments on

your feelings. There is no right or wrong about your feelings.

Feelings just are, and they need to be honored and given high

priority by you for your health. They have something to tell us

and we need to listen to them.

So my task for you is to practice this very thing and

learn to listen to your body and your emotions.

Take two minutes every day, and just sit still with your

eyes closed. Breathe deeply and slowly. Determine what you feel

... do you feel afraid, insecure, or worthless? Name the

emotions, and they will reward you by settling down and not

screaming anymore to be heard. When something comes up to

upset you, do not react instinctively by raging, cutting, eating or

whatever it is you do that is destructive to you or others.

Peace will begin to come to you.

It doesn't mean that things won't upset you anymore, but it

does mean that you will begin to have control over what upsets

you from now on. You can acknowledge that what someone

said or did, hurt you, and then let yourself feel it without

stuffing it down inside.

You cannot wish your feelings away, or say that you

shouldn't feel this or that. That is unrealistic and unhealthy.

And so begin today listening to yourself like you've never

listened before. Let's go through the exercise step by step.

Steps to Acknowledge Your Emotions

➥ Sit comfortably in a chair, or lie down.

➥ Close your eyes and breathe slowly and deeply.

- Focus on what parts of your body you are feeling - your legs, arms, torso, feet, hands, etc.

- Determine what emotion you are feeling.

- Focus on how and where you are feeling the emotion.

- Then, just let it be. Focus on it, listen to it, feel it.

That emotion should soon begin to fade away ... simply because it has been heard. You have listened to your emotions for the first time, like no one ever has, instead of ignoring them. Now you have the power to listen to yourself and nurture yourself when others will not or cannot. We want others to listen to us, but we have to listen to ourselves first and foremost.

It's up to you to listen to your feelings and acknowledge

them, and then express them to others. It is also up to you to

adjust a negative or destructive emotion to a different one that

makes you feel calm and content. No one else has the power to

determine what you feel. You alone are in control of your

emotions.

Listen to them!

Love and blessings,

~Barbara

My Commitment to

My Own Emotions

I am committed to letting my emotions have a place of

honor in my life. I want to learn to listen to my emotions,

acknowledge that they exist, and exist for a reason. I pledge to

take care of them so that I can heal from the pain.

I know this is a learning process and I am committed to

taking each new step along the way.

Every day is a new beginning.

Take a deep breath and start again

~Unknown

Step Four

Overcoming the Triggers

Something that I saw, or heard, or read ...

Something someone did or said to me...

Triggered me to feel a certain way or to recall a

time when I felt like this before.

What was it? Who did it? What happened?

Get to know what triggers you to feel overwhelmed and

in pain. Begin to list them here and when you realize a new one,

come back and post again. It will help you know what it is that

brings back flashbacks or bad memories, and will put you on

the path of knowing why your body and mind react the way

they do to certain things.

If you would like to share on the website, "Healing from

Abuse" (www.healingfromabuse.webs.com) not only are you

there to get help for your own healing, but your sharing will

bring healing to others. Isn't that a grand idea? That YOU, by

sharing your words, your thoughts, your feelings, can actually

help another human being ... You are needed there! We need

each other.

To overcome your triggers, you must do these things:

➥ Name the trigger – the event that made you feel a

certain way.

➥ Name the emotion that it stirs in you.

➤ Focus on the feeling, acknowledging it as you learned to

do in the earlier Healing Steps.

➤ Try to name the first time you felt that particular feeling

— can you connect it to a particular memory? Name that

memory, write it down, discard it from within you. Write it

here if you want, or put it in your own journal.

➤ Remember that it is ONLY a memory of a feeling, and

that memory cannot hurt you today, in the present.

➤ Continue to focus on the feeling, acknowledging it,

pinpointing it to a body sensation and letting it fade away.

➨ Repeat this, every time you experience a trigger. Tell

yourself that it is a MEMORY and not your present life. Stay

present; stay grounded.

➨ Write your triggers here. Keep track of what triggers

you and you will begin to see there is a pattern ... a pattern

you can break, if you learn to acknowledge them.

God has a plan for your life.

The enemy has a plan for your life.

Be ready for both.

Just be wise enough to know which one to battle

and which one to embrace.

Step Five

Who Failed You?

I want you to think about who failed you in your life. Who didn't give you the love and support that you needed? What did they do instead? What do you wish they had done? Who was it? Was it your friends, parents, grandparents, family...? Make a list and post it here.

Who failed me?

It is important to specifically name who and how people failed you. If you can't remember exact names of people from your past, for instance classmates, they could be listed as a group. Continue the list until you have listed everyone who has ever failed you in some way. It will help you get a clear picture of what has happened to you. Then you will begin to see what you can do to make a difference in your life ... for yourself, despite

what has been done to you.

My Commitment to

Overcoming Failed Relationships

The following people have failed me in my life. I was

depending on them to love and protect me, nurture me and

keep me from harm. They didn't do that for me. I was left

utterly alone to handle the abuse as best I knew how. I was not

capable, at my age, to handle what happened to me. An adult

was supposed to be looking out for me, but failed.

I am not to blame for my abuse. My abuser/s chose to take advantage of someone who could not defend themselves adequately and they knew it. These people failed me in my life and are to blame for my abuse. I will remember that it was not my fault that they abused me. I did nothing to deserve such treatment. No one deserves to be abused. No one. Not even me. No matter what they told me, no matter how much I believed it, I did not deserve to be abused. I will begin telling myself that every moment of every day until I believe it with my whole heart

...I DID NOT DESERVE TO BE ABUSED!!!!

As we grow up, we realize it becomes LESS important

To have more friends and MORE important

To have REAL friends.

Step Six

Facing the Reality

Now I want to tell you something, something that may be hard to hear. All of those people failed you – yes. It is a very sad thing when people you love fail you, especially in the ways they failed you. It is the reality of our lives. We can't change what other people have done to us, but we can change what we do now with it.

Simply facing the facts that these are the people who did these things to you is one step in getting closer to healing. It is in black and white, bold letters, plain and simple, that yes, that's what they did to you.

Now what I want you to do is write out your feelings about each one – about how they made you feel and how you feel about it today. Write out as much as you want ...it can be just stating what you feel, such as an emotion, or it can be in a letter format to each of them, about how they made you feel. Let it out. Release the feelings that are locked inside and get them out about each one that failed you.

You must face the reality of your life and what happened to you before you can move ahead and heal. Facing the reality of your life means getting the feelings out about what happened to you. Write it all out in your journal. You will feel a burden lift when you express the emotion inside. It has to be said. It has to be written. Let yourself feel the emotion. Let your

emotions be your friends.

My Commitment to

Facing Reality

Write a list of emotions that you feel when you think of

each person. Write a letter to each person expressing to him or

her how they failed you.

DON'T send the letter - just write it.

→ Note: The longer, the better. Get all the feelings that you

   can out on paper or computer screen. They need to be

   let out.

Enjoy the little things in life...

For one day you'll look back and realize they were the big things.

~Unknown

Step Seven

Disengage Emotionally

In order to heal, you MUST disengage from your abuser/s emotionally. You must cut the ties to them and not allow yourself to be an emotional puppet to them. Because of the abuse, they have connected themselves to your soul ... that's what abuse does to a person. Now it's up to you to cut those strings and break free of the emotional roller coaster they have you on. Try to disengage yourself from your abuser/s. Do not connect yourself with them emotionally. When you do, you break the control that they have over your emotions. It's like you have to believe that person doesn't exist, in your head, anyway. You just disregard them. They are on their own and you don't have to be part of their game. That helps make you free to make choices for yourself based on what YOU want and need instead of as a reaction to what someone else has done.

That actually is very important in taking back your life and healing. In the unhealthy way, we let other people determine for us what we are going to think and feel.

For instance:

"If she hadn't done that, I wouldn't feel this way."

"If he hadn't raped me, molested me, etc., I would not be all messed up."

"I wouldn't feel like this if it weren't for them."

On and on and on it goes, always letting someone else

make you feel a certain way. They don't have that right. YOU

decide how you are going to feel. YOU take charge of your

OWN life, emotions, and thoughts. It is not an easy process, but

once you make the choice to do that, it gets easier and easier as

you continually remind yourself that you, and you alone, decide

how you will feel at any given moment, no matter what has

happened to you in the past, or what happens to you in the

present.

Love and blessings,

~Barbara

My Commitment to

Disengage from my Abusers

I am choosing to stop the control that my abuser/s have

on me. I will no longer be their puppet emotionally. No one can

make me feel anything without my permission.

I choose to work on disengaging myself from my

abuser/s and others who make me feel bad about myself. I will

train my mind and heart and soul to know that my abuser/s do

not have control over me anymore.

I claim my emotional health back for ME. No one else

has it, no one else has the right to it, no on else can manipulate

me anymore.

I choose to feel what I feel, when I want to feel it.

I am committed to my healing and will do whatever it

takes to break free of this pain.

Now, it's YOUR emotional life! YOU choose to make of it

what you want!

Love to you,

~Barbara

We must be willing to let go of the life we have planned, so as to have the life that is waiting for us.

Step Eight

Learning to Self-Nurture

One of the things that tangles us up the most is that we long for

someone to take care of us, to hold

us, and make the pain go away. We have emptiness in our souls

where the love and nurturing should have taken place by those

we were entrusted to. Nothing can make up for what they failed

to give us, and our pain continues to eat away at us the more we

long for the person/s to love us the way we long to be loved.

But the logic has to follow:

If they didn't give us the kind of love and nurturing that

we needed when we were so little, when it could have shaped us

into healthy adults, how can we expect them to see that we still need it from them? It is illogical to think that they will

somehow change, and see the error of their ways and make up

for it?

If they didn't give it to us then, they won't give it to us

now, especially when we are living in "adult" bodies. Their

minds can't comprehend it. And so we are left to take care of

ourselves the way they were supposed to. I know it doesn't seem

fair and it doesn't feel like you are able to do such a thing, but

you must learn to do it.

You must learn to take yourself by the hand and lead

yourself into a calming, soothing place, a place where you will be

cuddled and held and loved, caressed and kissed, just for being you. You must find the ways that make you feel safe again,

loved, and nurtured. It is completely up to you; no on else can

do this for you. No parent, brother, or sister. No grandparents,

friends or teachers. No spouses. Only you.

That may sound lonely and it may be scary, but when it

comes right down to it, you need the strength to carry on your

life FOR you, BY you and no one else can do it FOR you. When

you are strong enough to take care of yourself, you will have

more of yourself to give, and you will begin to see that defining

who you are is completely up to you and you are not dependent

on anyone else for your survival, for you will have all of the

survival skills needed.

The following is a list of ways you can nurture yourself

when you are feeling badly. This of course, is not a complete list.

Pick and choose the ones you think will work for you and add

your own. Then refer back to your list when you need a way to

take care of the you who needs it so badly.

Self-Nurture Soothing Words, Affirmations

➤ Make a CD of affirmations. Have supportive people add

messages for you.

➤ Have a "Daily Bread Basket" of affirmations to read,

hold, and carry with you.

- Get a book of affirmations and carry it with you.

- Create a Healing Notebook: Put in affirmations, pictures, and messages from friends that remind you that you are safe and not alone. Carry the notebook with you wherever you go so that you can refer to it.

- Lucid Dreaming and Journaling: Use meditative and free-writing techniques. Write whatever comes to your mind. It can be anything.

- Self-Talk: Tell yourself something that will remind you that you are okay.

- Do a positive or nurturing spontaneous writing.

- Write affirmation cards or post-it notes.

- Journal about hopes and aspirations you have.

- Write a letter to yourself from someone who thinks

highly of you.

- With your non-dominant hand, write from the

perspective of your child self.

Soothing Deeds

- Get into cozy clothes.

- Get dressed up.

- Treat your body as you would a child who has been

injured and needs Tender Loving Care.

- Cook or bake something comforting.

- Take a hot bath.

➜ Take an oil or bubble bath.

➜ Light a candle or your fireplace.

➜ Soothe body memories: use lotion, essential oils, and soft

   fabric on places that hurt.

➜ Brush your hair.

➜ Rub your feet or hands.

➜ Buy yourself flowers or a houseplant.

➜ Buy yourself garden plants and plant them.

➜ Buy your inner child a coloring book.

➜ Have a cup of tea or hot chocolate.

➜ Have iced tea or lemonade.

➜ Have a chocolate or other comfort food.

- Buy something nice for yourself or your house.

- Spend time with your cat or dog.

- Listen to music.

- Read a children's book.

- Read your favorite author or book, just for fun.

Healthy Things to Do

- Mend clothes.

- Rearrange your furniture.

- Decorate a room.

- Time out: Put thoughts and feelings to the back of your

  mind, by distracting yourself and staying busy.

- Count to 10.

- Make and put up a joy list.

- Play with a small child.

- Watch a sunrise or sunset.

- Go someplace you enjoy.

- Go somewhere with a friend.

- Go to a place with a fountain, waterfall, beach, stream,

  lake or nature trail.

Art forms

- Blow bubbles.

- Play a card game.

- Make a collage.

- Make artwork.

- Sing to your favorite music.

- Watch a comedy on TV.

- Make a scrapbook with inspirational and empowering

  images and quotes.

- Go to a playground and swing or use the jungle gym.

- Learn to laugh at yourself.

- Play hopscotch or darts.

Taking Care of Yourself

- Get sleep if you need it.

- Use aromatherapy.

- Get a facial or a massage.

➥ Eat something good for you.

➥ Go for a walk.

➥ Listen to what your body needs.

➥ Ask yourself if you need to eat.

Physical Release

➥ Exercise or dance to expressive music.

➥ Jog or run.

➥ Go skating.

➥ Lift weights.

➥ Sing really loud.

➥ Run around and play.

➥ Go sledding, ride a bike or swim.

➡ Clean the house.

➡ Clang pots and pans

➡ Put on music and play drums or bongos.

➡ Go out and kick a ball.

➡ Use a punching bag.

➡ Punch a pillow.

➡ Shake your body; allow the fear, hurt or anger to shake

out of your arms and legs.

➡ Allow yourself to cry or moan in a safe, supportive place.

➡ Breathe deeply to release heavy pain in the chest.

➡ Go somewhere safe and scream.

➡ Scream into a pillow.

- Stamp your feet.

- Pound something with a tube, hose or foam bat.

- Wring a towel.

- Use a stress ball.

- Tear up newspaper, cardboard or a telephone book.

- Build something with a hammer.

- Trim the hedge.

- Throw rocks in the water.

- Squeeze or pound clay.

- Have a pillow or marshmallow fight.

- Rock in a comfortable rocking chair

- Make a list of your dreams for the future

- Make a quilt

- Shine your sink

- Crochet or knit

- Call a friend just to chat

- Write in your journal

- Sleep as long as you want

.

My Commitment to

Taking Care of Myself

I am committed to taking care of myself. I will learn to

nurture and soothe myself whenever I feel overwhelmed with

pain and grief. It is up to me alone to take care of myself. I am

very important to myself. I am the only one of me and that's

what I will have the rest of my life. I am committed to making

sure that I am well-fed and well taken care of in every possible

way in order to lead a productive and healthy life.

I choose the following things to nurture and soothe

myself when I need to:

 _____

_____

_____

I already do things to nurture and soothe myself and I

am proud of myself for doing these things for me!

I will remember to do these things on a day-to-day basis

... because I am worth every minute of it.

I love myself.

When something bad happens
You have three choices. You
Can either let it define you, or you
Can let it strengthen you.

Step Nine

Write a Letter to Your Inner

Child

You have to reach her. You have to find her. You have to rescue her. You have to be the one to take care of her. You're the only one who can.

I want you to think about the pain within you, and how much of it is from a little girl crying because someone hurt her, or her needs were not met, or whatever it was that caused all of the pain in the first place. Think about the little girl that you were when it happened and what that little girl felt like back then.

I want you to talk to her. Tell her that you will be here for her from now on and that no one can hurt her anymore. Tell her that you want to listen to her and have her tell you how she feels and what she thinks. Tell her that she is precious and

deserves all of the good things that she should have had before

all of the pain set it. Tell her that you are going to work on

bringing those good things to her now and making sure she has

everything she needs or wants. She's waiting to talk to you.

Love and blessings

~Barbara

Write a Letter to Your Inner Child

Begin the letter something like this:

"My dear inner child ...

I want to hear you. I want to

listen to you. I want to know what it is that makes you

feel the most pain and makes you the saddest. Please

talk to me. Please tell me. I am here for you..."

Then listen to what she tells you. Write it down. Make

it a conversation. Share it on the online support group. It will

make you feel better to know there are others who know exactly what you mean and understand where you are. We are here for

each other, and you are here to take care of you too.

Love and blessings,

~Barbara

You're amazing

Just the way you are.

Step Ten

Knowing There is a Higher Power

I know the confusion. You have a lot of garbage to get rid of. And it is a very lonely road. I will never claim that asking God into your life will get rid of the pain. It will never take everything away and make you a person that was never abused and broken. You are broken. All of us who have been abused are broken. Each and every person on this Earth is broken in one way or another. It takes more than going to church or praying a single prayer to heal all of your pain. This will take a life-long existence of dealing with the brokenness, to heal from it. As I have said before, it will not be overnight.

What I am saying to you though, is that asking God to

come into your life, asking for His forgiveness for your part in

being a sinner (because all of us, including you, were born as

sinners) and asking forgiveness for everything that you have

done wrong and telling Him that you want Him in your life,

because you have faith in Him and believe that He wants ONLY

good for you. If you will trust Him, making that kind of choice

and acting on it WILL make a difference in your life, simply

because He gives:

➴ Hope to the hopeless

➴ Love to the loveless

➴ Mercy to the merciless

➜ Understanding to the misunderstood

➜ Healing to the broken...

...and so much more. Most of all, He'll never leave you, abandon you or betray you! That's incredible to think about! You'll never be alone in this world when you have God's Spirit living inside of you. You can talk to Him whenever you want, and He'll listen. He'll converse with you, as real conversations, as a really still quiet voice within your own spirit. He will direct you, guide you and protect you ... if you'll only let Him.

The thing is, you have to ask for it. You have to reach out YOUR hand and heart to His because He is already holding out His hand to yours. You have to grab hold of it. You have to

say in your heart:

"Lord, take me, I'm yours! Forgive me for all of the sins I've

committed and wash me clean! I want you in my life forever

and ever. I don't understand all of this, but I am willing to have

you teach me and I'm willing to learn. I believe you died on the

cross for me personally to give me a beautiful life that I'd never

have otherwise, and to be able to spend eternity with you in

Heaven. Please help me. I need you."

He'll answer your prayer and be with you, because He

promises to. I think the cool thing about it is that we have to

respond to Him – He already has asked us to be loved by Him, and He's waiting for us to accept that or reject it. What is even

cooler is that He will NEVER force His love on us, and do you

know why? Because He wants it to be OUR choice. Otherwise, He

wouldn't be any different than our abusers who only wanted to

take for themselves. He wants to give His love to you – His perfect

love! Not anything like what you have experienced. He's just

waiting for you to say YES to Him, because you trust Him. That's

it!

I think it is incredible how God works in our lives. I think it is

just amazing what He does. I can't explain it; I don't have

words for it, but its there, and you know it when He's there.

HE loves you. He LOVES you. Jesus loves YOU.

GOD LOVES YOU!

You are very, very precious to Him. He wants you as His own

child. Let Him adopt you into His family because your family

does not have everything you need from them. He's just waiting

for you to make that decision. Decide today.

Love and blessings,

~Barbara

P.S. Hang in there! You will heal! You will overcome this!

Because you are worth it all!

My Commitment to God

I realize that I need you, God, and that I need You in my

life. I can't do this life without you. I understand that You sent

Jesus to die for me so that I could live with you forever and so

that I could be adopted into your family. I want to be in your

family where you can love me like I need to be loved because my

family really stinks and I know that I will never receive from

them what I want and need. Only you know what I need,

because you created me and You know my deepest thoughts,

longings, and needs. I believe that You can provide everything

for me that I need. My life is so lacking right now, and I know that if you come into my life and heart that you will guide me,

protect me, and give me everything I possibly could need. I

know life won't be perfect, and that it will still have pain and

difficulties, but at least I know that you are with me, and that

alone, gives me comfort.

I ask you into my life to be with me forever and I will

commit myself to learning more about your great love for me

and how I need to live my life so that it does not destroy me. I

turn my back on Satan and his ways and I choose to follow You

– because you are everything good and right and pure and

holy. I want that in my life. I want the kind of depth of love that only You can reach within me. I want to be healed of my

pain, and I believe that you can heal me.

I will love you, God, and Your Son, Jesus, because you

first loved me. I will choose to love you back, because that

means that I can have a real relationship with you and that I

can talk to you and you will talk to me and you will never leave

me.

So please, right now, please come into my heart and live

with me forever and guide me through this life because it is so

painful here and I need you with me. I want you. I will commit

to learning more about you and what you have for me. I want to know. Help me to understand as I stumble along on this path,

because I really don't know what to do.

Thank you, God. Thank you, Jesus, for coming into my

heart. I believe you when you say that you will. I love you, Lord

Jesus!

In Jesus' name, I love you, Lord. Amen and Amen!

"For God so loved the world that He gave His only Son, that whoever believes in Him should not perish, but have everlasting life."

-John 3:16 KJV (paraphrased)

Reading the Word

If you choose to make this commitment, then go out and

purchase a version of the Bible that catches your eye and is

understandable to you. There are some great ones out on the

market. Check out the bookstores in your area for the one

that is right for you.

Then read it every day and find out what God wants to

say to you. What I think is awesome is that you pick up your

Bible and pray, "Lord, show me what you want me to know today", then open it up randomly. Start reading, and don't stop until something really speaks to you. If you don't find it on the page opened, then leaf through it again, searching for something that catches your heart and causes it to stop or leap with an excitement that you've never felt before, because it will be there. Read until you find that special word, phrase, sentence, or paragraph, and then stop and let that just soak into your being. It will stay with you during the day and because God will cause you to think about it and remember it and you will begin to understand and feel things that you never have before.

It's an awesome journey in itself. I hope you choose to

take it!

It is better to let someone

Walk away from you than all over you.

My Commitment to Reading and Studying the Bible

I commit myself to reading the Bible every day to find

peace and contentment and solutions to my problems. I will

keep this up a week at a time, not to overwhelm myself, and

continue as I am able. I commit to praying every day to Jesus

who will take my prayers and petitions to God, and I will trust

that God will answer my prayers - in His own perfect time.

"Give your entire attention to what God is doing right now, and don't get worked up about what may or may not happen tomorrow. God will help you deal with whatever hard things come up when the time comes."

~Matthew 6:34, THE MESSAGE

"Is it ever finished? Probably not. We cannot leave our losses behind; they stay with us, growing into our lives. But eventually we carry them – they no longer carry us. As time, like the tide, smoothes their contours, we find a smaller, more comfortable place for them. Looking back, we can recognize the sea changes between then and now."

(Words I Never Thought to Speak, by Victoria Alexander, pg. 232)

When someone says "You've changed"

It simply means you've stopped

Living your life their way.

You're amazing just the way you are.

Chapter Eleven

Believing the Truth about Yourself

1t is important to believe the truth about yourself. There

are so many lies that you're believing right now that you

can't possibly stand alone in your self-worth. You must

recognize the lies within you that are rotting your very soul.

These lies sound something like this:

"Nobody loves me, everybody hates me; guess I'll go eat worms."

"I am not worthy of love."

"I'm so ugly; nobody can love a person like me."

"I can't trust anyone."

"No one understands me."

"I am alone in this world."

And the list goes on and on. I know this is very difficult, but you will feel much better when you recognize that all of those negative things you are believing are coming from Satan, the father of lies himself and he wants nothing more than to destroy

you with his lies.

Write out all of the negative things you are telling yourself.

Then let the Light shine into your soul and write down the

opposite of what you are believing. It will be slow, but start

believing the Truth about yourself and you will become a different

person—lively, loving, peaceful, and calm.

Dearly beloved, avenge not yourselves, but rather give place to wrath: for it is written, Vengeance is mine; I will repay, says the Lord.

Romans 12:19 KJV (Paraphrased)

Chapter Twelve

Forgiveness

I know that this step seems impossible, and in some ways, it is. You've been hurt so deeply that the last thing on your mind is to forgive the one/s who harmed you. You feel guilty for not forgiving them, but in your heart, you know that you just aren't ready for that. I understand. People tell you to just get over it, but it isn't that simple. It takes time and effort to get past the damage to your soul. I urge you, don't feel guilty for not forgiving your abuser/s. It will take quite a while to get to the point where you can forgive; in fact, as I experienced, it was one of the last steps I took that brought healing to my spirit and soul. You don't need to rush it. God will lead you to that quiet and peaceful place in His time.

The act of forgiveness is a decision. My forgiveness came as a still, small voice, showing me the Truth about my abuser/s and what God thought of them. I was taken aback at this new truth, and it came so softly that it changed my life.

The Spirit of the Lord spoke to me as I stood in church singing songs to my Savior. I had prayed many times, "Lord, how can I handle all of this pain? It's much too great to bear alone."

And then I heard in my spirit, "Barb, you don't have to bear it alone; I am here to help you. I have come to take away your pain because you are too small to carry it. You do not have the strength or the know-how to deal with this burden. I forgave you of your sins many years ago, and I have come to bring peace and contentment for you. I have died on the cross and have borne all

of your heavy sins upon myself so that you could live free. I have

also died for your abuser/s so that they may do the same. But

more importantly, to you, at this place, is that I died on that cross

to bear the sins of your abusers and what they did to you and

have taken the burden of their sins away from you to free you

from the awful weight of their sins. It's a miracle! All you have to

do is accept it, and then you can forgive your abuser/s."

And so I did that day, and I suddenly knew that I didn't need

to carry the weight of my pain any longer; Jesus had died on the

cross to take that burden away. I was as light as a feather from that time on. The issue of forgiveness had been taken care of and

I was free to love my abuser/s in spite of what they did to me.

I hurt myself today to see if I still feel.

I focus on the pain — the only thing that's real.

~ Nine Inch Nails

Part II

The Survivor Diaries

Daily Steps in Healing

I wrote this book to assist me in my own

healing journey. With the help of my therapist, I

started to learn how to take charge of my

emotions and not let them control me. I learned

that triggers aren't fatal and that they slowly fade

away. And I learned that all of my experiences could become friends, and I could find peace and healing after all.

And so I share it with you.

Grab a notebook or other contained book that you can use for journaling. This is your diary for you to keep. You are free to write as little or as much as you want, and express exactly what you want without anyone holding you back. You have permission to tell your story and tell the secrets here. If you are in therapy now, I suggest you use it in conjunction with what your therapist is working on with you. If you aren't in therapy, this will be a start to get in touch with who you were before and after the abuse started and stopped. This book is not intended to replace therapy. Please find professional help to

deal with your issues.

Write in your diary every day throughout

the year. If it gets overwhelming, stop and take a

break. Then come back when you have a fresher

view. It is my hope and prayer that some of the

pain of abuse will subside for you and that this

book will lead you to a new journey on your

healing path.

The Survivor Diaries is a self-help

instructional tool to aid in the healing of those

dealing with the after-effects of emotional,

physical, and sexual abuse. This is your diary to

write your innermost hurts and pain. This book

is meant to work through the daily steps of

taking care of yourself, little by little, honoring

your feelings, your emotions, and your own

body sensations. It is to help you through the overwhelming pain and find freedom in knowing the truth about yourself and your abuse experiences.

There are only 10 topics to respond to. Hopefully that will make it easy enough for you to complete every day and come back tomorrow to do all over again. In order to heal from the pain of abuse, you must be proactive in bringing about that healing. Please respond to the steps listed here and follow the instructions given. This will be your own diary of your day-to-day survival, which can become your road to freedom. This is your handbook to return to every day to enter your progress, and see how far you have come in your own healing journey. Follow the steps each day to find peace, comfort, and a new sense of self-worth...

... because you are worth every minute of it.

Love and blessings,

~Barbara

Step One

Morning wake-up

What time did you wake up?

_____

_____

_____

_____

_____

_____

How many hours of sleep did you get?

_____

_____

_____

_____

_____

_____

_____

_____

_____

_____

_____

_____

_____

Was it restful sleep?

_____

_____

_____

_____

_____

_____

_____

_____

_____

_____

_____

_____

_____

_____

How did you feel when you woke up?

_____

_____

_____

_____

_____

_____

_____

_____

_____

_____

_____

_____

Describe yourself as you face the new day -

who are you today?

_____

_____

_____

_____

_____

_____

_____

_____

_____

_____

_____

_____

_____

Do you notice any particular body

sensations - what is your body telling you

today?

_____

_____

_____

_____

_____

_____

_____

_____

_____

_____

_____

Step Two

Reflections of the Night

Take a moment and think about what your

sleep was like last night.

Was it restful sleep?

_____

_____

_____

_____

_____

_____

_____

_____

_____

_____

_____

_____

_____

_____

Did you have any dreams?

_____

_____

_____

_____

_____

_____

_____

_____

_____

_____

_____

_____

_____

_____

Did you have any nightmares?

_____

_____

_____

_____

_____

_____

_____

_____

_____

_____

_____

_____

_____

Describe your dreams / nightmares here,

taking note of the feelings that come up, the

details of the dream / nightmare, and any

symbolic significance of them.

_____

_____

_____

_____

_____

_____

_____

_____

_____

_____

_____

What kind of message do you feel was being
expressed in your dream / nightmare?

_____

_____

_____

_____

_____

_____

_____

_____

_____

_____

_____

_____

_____

Step Three

Start the day.

Today is a new day. You can choose to be

whatever you want to do and be today.

What is it that you need to do?

_____

_____

_____

_____

_____

_____

_____

_____

_____

_____

_____

_____

_____

What are your thoughts about who you are

today?

_____

_____

_____

_____

_____

_____

_____

_____

_____

_____

_____

_____

_____

What are the feelings that accompany those

thoughts?

_____

_____

_____

_____

_____

_____

_____

_____

_____

_____

_____

_____

Step Four

Daily Tasks

Checklist for daily tasks: personal hygiene,

housework chores, work, etc. Personalize it

to your own needs.

_____

_____

_____

_____

Step Five

Who are you?

Who do you want to be?

It is easy to believe that you are worthless, unloved, betrayed, lost, a non-person, but you aren't. You are not what someone did to you. That does not define you. Neither is any illness you "caught" when this happened to you. You are a lovely, loving, beautiful, giving person who wants to come out, but without all of the fear it brings. I want you to think about who you are, who you really are, deep down, when it's just you. Write that down. You can add to it as you go along. Next, I want you to write down what you wish you were, or who you want to be.

You can become that if you want to work toward it. Now think about what you have to do and say to make you that person, without all of the pain. You can do it. It just takes practice. Don't ever give up.

_____

_____

_____

_____

Step Six

Self-Soothing Things to Do

You have a great need within to take

care of yourself, soothe yourself, comfort

yourself and make everything ok again. You

are the only one who can do this for yourself

if you want to break free of the pain. No one

else can do it for you.

What do you do to nurture and soothe

yourself?

_____

_____

_____

_____

_____

_____

_____

_____

_____

_____

_____

_____

_____

Did you do any of these things today? What
did you do?

_____

_____

_____

_____

_____

_____

_____

_____

_____

_____

_____

_____

_____

_____

_____

A few suggestions: Please add your own

- Sit alone in your rocking chair

- Sleep

- Take a hot bath or shower

- Fill your birdfeeders and watch the birds

- Talk and listen to your children

- Talk and listen to your husband

- Play some good music

- Blog, write in your journal or read posts in your online groups

- Respond to message & letters from others

- Send an email to your therapist to tell her what is going on with you

- Clean the house, especially the dishes and floors

Did you do any of these things today?

_____

_____

_____

_____

_____

_____

_____

_____

_____

_____

_____

_____

_____

_____

Step Seven

The Child Within

I remember that I would use this a lot

while working through all of my issues ...

taking care of the little girl/boy within who is

scared, can't talk, wants to cry or sleep all day

long, and is being ignored. I would have to

mentally talk to the small one/s within me

and tell them what they needed to hear and

believe - that I was there for them now and I wouldn't let anything happen to them anymore; that they could trust me and that I would listen to everything they had to say. This can happen periodically throughout the day – whenever the overwhelming feelings of being "lost" or not knowing what to do or how to express something, or anger ... a whole myriad of emotions/feelings that come up.

It's up to you to nurture that little child within you and take care of him/her the way she/he was supposed to be taken care of in the first place. This may take practice for you at first, but once you get the hang of recognizing that the little one's needs within you are not being met, then the adult part of you can take care of it. It's the only healthy thing to do. So decide how you want to take care of that little person and do it ... for him/her and for yourself.

Did you feel like a little child yearning to be taken care of, held, rocked, listened to, snuggled with, kissed, and nurtured today?

Explain.

What brought up those feeling?

_____

_____

_____

_____

_____

_____

_____

_____

_____

What do you wish someone would do for

you at these times?

_____

_____

_____

_____

_____

_____

_____

_____

_____

_____

_____

_____

_____

Imagine a little child standing in front of you, feeling the same way you are feeling, needing to be taken care of. What would you do for that child? What would you say?

_____

_____

_____

_____

_____

_____

_____

_____

_____

_____

_____

Now write a letter to the child that is you standing in front of you and take care of him/her the way you would take care of any other child that desperately needed something from you.

What are you going to do for the child within you today to help him/her feel nurtured and cared for?

_____

_____

_____

_____

_____

_____

_____

_____

_____

_____

What did you do today for the child within,

inside of you?

_____

_____

_____

_____

_____

_____

_____

_____

_____

_____

_____

_____

_____

_____

Step Eight

EMOTIONS:

Did you experience any specific emotions

today? What were they?

_____

_____

_____

_____

_____

_____

EXPERIENCES

What experiences brought these emotions to

the surface?

_____

_____

_____

_____

_____

_____

_____

_____

_____

_____

_____

_____

_____

THOUGHTS

What particular thoughts were troubling you

today?

_____

_____

_____

_____

_____

_____

_____

_____

_____

_____

_____

_____

_____

What experiences brought on these thoughts?

_____

_____

_____

_____

_____

_____

_____

_____

_____

_____

_____

_____

_____

_____

TRIGGERS

What particular things triggered memories

and flashbacks today?

_____

_____

_____

_____

_____

_____

_____

_____

_____

_____

_____

_____

_____

What was the memory or flashback?

Describe it in detail.

_____

_____

_____

_____

_____

_____

_____

_____

_____

_____

_____

_____

_____

_____

_____

Step Nine

Self-Destruction

We do lots of things to self-destruct: cutting,

drugs, alcohol, suicidal thoughts, overeating,

etc. ... most of it is brought on by an

overwhelming sense of pain and the need to

escape it all. Think about what brings those

feelings up within you... What do you do to

self-destruct or self-injure?

How often did you do something today to

hurt yourself?

_____

_____

_____

_____

_____

_____

_____

_____

_____

_____

_____

_____

What brought on the urge to hurt yourself?

_____

_____

_____

_____

_____

_____

_____

_____

_____

_____

_____

_____

_____

_____

Who was involved? What were the feelings

that surfaced?

_____

_____

_____

_____

_____

_____

_____

_____

_____

_____

_____

_____

_____

Step Ten

Getting the Story Out

Using a journal, write your story, little bits at a time or as much as you can. Take your time and allow yourself to heal as you regurgitate it.

_____

_____

_____

_____

Congratulations!

You are on the road to healing from

the atrocity of abuse.

You will be interested in knowing that
you are living your life in a cycle. You have
good days and bad days. It is important to
track yourself every day so that you can be
aware of what is probably going to come
about for you day to day. Give yourself a
break when you are not feeling the best, and
go ahead and tackle a lot of things when you
have energy and a good attitude. But
remember, bad days will come back. You just
have to take each day as it comes and realize
that it is only a day; it is not forever. Slowly

you will make progress in how much you can accomplish during the day.

I hope this little book helped you find the child within you and heal that child for the first time in his/her life. You are the catalyst for that healing. This book is not meant to replace therapy. Please find a professional who can walk you through whatever you are dealing with.

Now go in peace, live your life to the fullest, and may God bless you in all you do. Go and be a blessing in someone else's life who is hurting today.

Love and blessings,

~Barbara

P.S. I would LOVE to hear from you! Email, write or call to let me know how God has blessed your life on your healing journey. Contact information is in the back of the book.

Congratulations!

I'm so proud of you.

You've have come so far on

Your healing journey!

Now, go be a blessing

To others who are hurting.

   Love and Blessings,

   ~Barbara E. Kompik

Comfort Food Recipes

I know how hard it can be to get out of bed and simply make something to eat. I know because I was there too. So I have included a little collection of comfort foods that are easy to make and simply delicious. I hope you enjoy them as much as I have over the years.

Easy Salads

Grandma Hilda's Bananas & Sauce

1 Bunch of bananas
1 C. Mayonnaise
½ C. Sugar
1-2 T. Mustard

Mix together the sauce. It should be sweet and tangy. Adjust recipe if needed. Pour over sliced bananas. Great as a snack or with a meal!

Grandma Ida's Lemon Gelatin Salad

My Grandma Ida would make this at Thanksgiving or Christmas when we had our holiday meal. It was a favorite then and still is today as our family has grown. This is one of our family traditions.

Mix together:
2 pkg. lemon Gelatin, cooked and set partially.
2 sliced bananas
½ C min-marshmallows
1 can crushed pineapple, saving the juice

Cook together then cool completely.

Pineapple juice and water to make 1 C.
½ C sugar
2 T. flour
2 T. butter

When the sauce is cooled, add 1 container of Cool Whip. Top with 1 C shredded cheddar cheese. Don't forget the cheese! It makes this salad special.

Grandma Ida's and Mom's
Fresh Cucumber Slices

This is a real treat in the summertime when the garden vegetables are ripe. I could eat these all summer long.

Soak in salt water for ½ hour:

1 cucumber, thinly sliced
½ large white onion, sliced and separated

Boil together:

¼ C vinegar
¾ C water
2/3 C. sugar

Cool completely. Drain the salt water off of the vegetables, then pour syrup over them. Seal in a container. Set over night to let the flavors mingle.

Quick Fruit Salad

This is a winner when you feel like something
sweet but don't have the gumption to cook
or bake. So easy!

1 C drained crushed pineapple
1 C mandarin oranges, drained
1 C flaked coconut
1 C mini marshmallows
1 C cool whip
½ C maraschino cherries, drained
Your favorite nut pieces

Mix and chill, and that's it!

Seven Layer Salad

Layer in cake pan or glass bowl in this order:

1 head lettuce, chopped
Green or purple onion, chopped
1 can water chestnuts, drained
1 small pkg. frozen green peas
1 C mayonnaise
Sprinkled bacon bits
1 C. shredded cheddar cheese

Mom's Cherry Waldorf Salad

Dissolve together:

1 8 oz. pkg. cherry Gelatin
2 C boiling water

Add enough ice to cool thoroughly.

Add:

2 – 3 chopped apples
1 – 2 stalks chopped celery

Chill to set.

Macaroni Salad

8 oz cooked elbow macaroni
1 lb. Hot dogs, cooked and sliced
1 C mayonnaise
½ C cubed American cheese
1 T prepared mustard
½ t. salt
¼ t. pepper
3 – 4 pinches of paprika
1 T. celery seed

Toss, cover, and chill. Makes eight cups.

Anita's Spaghetti Salad

1 16 oz. pkg. spaghetti, cooked, drained, and chilled
1 onion, finely chopped
1 green pepper, finely chopped
2 tomatoes, diced
1 cucumber, diced
1 c. Italian salad dressing
2 T. salad seasonings

Combine ingredients. Add tomatoes and cucumber just before serving.

Maxine's Fruit Salad

Assorted fresh fruit chopped:

Apples, bananas, raspberries, cherries, blueberries

Add:

1 pkg. Instant vanilla or lemon pudding
1 C Milk
1 small carton whipped cream

Fold in fruit. Garnish with raspberries on top. Chill and serve.

Charlotte' Cole Slaw

Shred together:

1 head cabbage
2 carrots
1 small onion

Boil hard for 2 minutes:

2 C sugar
1 C vinegar
½ C water

Add:

1 t. celery seed
1 t. salt
¼ t. pepper
1 C oil

Cool sauce. Pour over cabbage.

This is a great picnic salad, beautifully colorful.

Cranberry Gelatin Salad

Cook:

½ pkg. Cranberries
½ C. water
½ C. sugar

Add:

2 pkg. Red raspberry gelatin
½ c. orange juice

Dice:

2 apples
2 stalks celery

Add:

½ C chopped pecans

Thanksgiving wouldn't have been the same
without this perky salad.

Patty's Easy Salad

1 lg. Cool Whip
1 can cherry pie filling
1 can crushed pineapple
1 can sweetened condensed milk
1 C chopped pecans

Stir up in large bowl. Chill. Serve.

Rainbow Fruit Salad

Layer in glass bowl in this order:

1 large mango, peeled & diced
2 C fresh blueberries
2 bananas, sliced
2 C fresh strawberries, halved
2 C seedless green grapes
2 nectarines, peeled & sliced

Honey Orange Sauce

(Sauce for Rainbow Salad)

1/3 C unsweetened orange juice
2 T lemon juice
1 ½ T. honey
¼ t. ground ginger
Dash nutmeg

Combine and stir. Just before serving, pour
over fruit.
Makes 12 servings.

Leslie's Candied Nuts

Mix together:
½ C sugar
1 T. cinnamon
¼ t. salt
Whisk in large bowl:
1 egg white
1 T. cold water
Add to egg white mixture until coated:
1 lb. Pecans
Then add to sugar mixture.

Bake at 225 degrees 1 hour. Stir every 20 minutes.

Grandma Ida's Candied Apples

Melt 3 T butter in a skillet. Slice 3 – 4 tart apples and place into skillet. Sprinkle hot cinnamon candies over top. (Red Hots) Add water and sugar. Cook slowly on simmer.

3 lb. Jonathon applies
1 pkg. Red Hoots
1 ½ C sugar
2 C. water

Save juice and use for a simple gelatin salad, preferably a red flavor.

Dad's Macaroni-Tomato Bake

A couple handfuls of uncooked macaroni
1 can diced tomatoes with juice
Salt to taste
¼ C sugar

Cook macaroni, drain. Stir in tomatoes, salt, and sugar.
Bake @ 350 degrees 45 minutes or until bubbly.

Main Dishes

Grandma Ida's Meatloaf

1 lb. Ground Hamburger
1 C. Chili Sauce
1 C. Quick Quaker Oats

Mix together and place in a loaf pan. Bake in the oven at 350 degrees for 30-45 minutes until done.

Suggested Meal: Cheesy Potatoes, Grandma Ida's Gelatin Salad, and your choice of vegetable. Wonderful as a Sunday meal.

Mom's Sloppy Joes

1 lb. Ground Hamburger, cooked & drained
2 T. Ketchup
2 T. Mustard
2 T. Brown Sugar
2 T. white Vinegar

Mix together and bring to boil. Put on top of hamburger buns.

Mom's Cheesy Potatoes

6 potatoes, peeled, and thinly sliced
1 can cream of celery soup
1 can cheddar cheese soup
2 cans milk
Milk to cover

Mix the 2 cans of soup and 2 cans of milk together. Gently stir into the sliced potatoes. Pour into greased casserole dish and cover with milk just to the top edges of the potatoes.

Bake at 350 for one hour or until potatoes are tender to a fork.

For a main dish, add cubed ham or sliced hot dogs. Always a favorite!

Mom Kompik's Quiche

12 slices bacon, cooked
1 C cheese
1/3 C onion
Place in bottom on 9x13 pan

Mix:

2 C milk
½ C Bisques
4 eggs
salt and pepper to taste.

Bake @ 350 degrees for 50 – 55 minutes.

May substitute ham or sausage for bacon.
Great at potlucks or church breakfasts.

Taco Casserole

1 pkg. crescent rolls
1 small pkg. tortilla chips, crushed
1 small carton sour cream
1 C shredded cheddar cheese
1 lb. Hamburger, cooked & drained
1 pkg. taco seasoning
Chopped lettuce
Chopped tomato

Brown meat, add taco seasoning and ½ c water; simmer. Mix sour cream into meat. Place rolls in 9 x 13 dish and press ½ of the chips into the rolls. Pour meat overtop. Sprinkle cheese and rest of chips over the top. Bake at 375 degrees 25 minutes. Serve with chopped lettuce and tomatoes.

Easy Hamburger Sandwiches

1 loaf French bread
1 lb. Hamburger, cooked
Garlic butter
Mozzarella cheese

Slice bread loaf in ½ length-wise. Spread
with garlic butter. Top with cooked
hamburger. Sprinkle shredded mozzarella
cheese on top. Bake 350 degrees for 10 – 15
minutes until cheese melts.

Spaghetti Pie

Combine:
1 lb. Ground hamburger, cooked and drained
1 jar of your favorite spaghetti sauce

Stir together:
½ small box of spaghetti, cooked and drained
1 egg, whisked
1 C Parmesan cheese

1 C. Mozzarella cheese

Place spaghetti mixture into the bottom and sides of pie pan, shape into crust. Pour sauce mixture into the center of the spaghetti. Top with mozzarella cheese. Bake @ 350 degrees for 20 minutes. Makes 6 servings.

Chip Dip

1 lb hamburger
1 lb. Velveeta cheese
1 lb. Pork and beans
1 Can evaporated milk

Brown meat, season with onion, garlic, green
pepper – optional.
Add cheese and milk. Melt. Add beans.
Serve hot with tortilla chips.

This is good to cook in the crock pot.

Survivors Bill of Rights
Author Unknown

As a Matter of Personal AUTHORITY, You Have the Right ...

...to manage your life according to your own values and judgment

...to direct your recovery, answerable to no one for your goals, effort, or progress

...to gather information to make intelligent decisions about your recovery

...to seek help from a variety of sources, unhindered by demands for exclusivity

...to decline help from anyone without having to justify the decision

...to have faith in your powers of self restoration -- and to seek allies who share it

...to trust allies in healing as much as any adult can trust another, but no more

...to be afraid and to avoid what frightens you

...to decide for yourself whether, when, and where to confront your fear

...to learn by experimenting, that is, to make mistakes.

For the Preservation of Personal BOUNDARIES, You Have the Right ...

...to be touched only with your permission, and only in ways that are comfortable

...to choose to speak or remain silent, about any topic or at any moment

...to choose to accept or decline feedback, suggestions, or interpretations

...to ask for help in healing, without having to accept help with work, play, or love

...to challenge any crossing of your boundaries

...to take appropriate action to end any

trespass that does not cease when challenged. In the Sphere of Personal COMMUNICATION, You Have the Right ...

...to ask for explanation of communications you do not understand

...to express a contrary view when you do understand and you disagree

...to acknowledge your feelings, without having to justify them as assertions of fact or actions affecting others

...to ask for changes when your needs are not being met

...to speak of your experience, with respect for your doubts and uncertainties

...to resolve doubt without deferring to the views or wishes of anyone. Specific to the DOMAIN of Psychotherapy, You Have the Right ...

...to hire a therapist or counselor as coach, not boss, of your recovery

...to receive expert and faithful assistance in healing from your therapist

...to be assured that your therapist will refuse to engage in any other relationship with you -

-business, social, or sexual -- for life

...to be secure against revelation of anything you have disclosed to your therapist, unless a court of law commands it

...to have your therapist's undivided loyalty in relation to any and all perpetrators, abusers, or oppressors

...to receive informative answers to questions about your condition, your hopes for recovery, the goals and methods of treatment, the therapist's qualifications

...to have a strong interest by your therapist in your safety, with a readiness to use all legal means to neutralize an imminent threat to your life or someone else's

...to have your therapist's commitment to you not depend on your "good behavior," unless criminal activity or ongoing threats to safety are involved

...to know reliably the times of sessions and of your therapist's availability, including, if you so desire, a commitment to work together for a set term

...to telephone your therapist between regular scheduled sessions, in urgent need, and have the call returned within a reasonable time

...to be taught skills that lessen risk of retraumatization containment (reliable temporal/spatial boundaries for recovery work);(b) systematic relaxation;(c) control of attention and imagery (through trance or other techniques)

...to reasonable physical comfort during sessions.

What We Would Like You

To Know About Us

Author Unknown

1. We grew up feeling very isolated and vulnerable, a feeling that continues into our adult lives.

2. Our early development has been interrupted by abuse, which either holds us back or pushes us ahead developmentally.

3. Sexual abuse has influenced all parts of our lives. Not dealing with it is like ignoring an open wound. Our communication style, our self-confidence, and our trust levels are affected.

4. Putting thoughts and feelings related to our abuse "on the back burner" does not make them go away. The only way out is to go through these emotions and process them.

5. Our interest in sexual activity will usually decline while we are dealing with this early trauma. This is because:

---we are working on separating the past from the present.
---pleasure and pain can sometimes be experienced simultaneously.
--- it is important for us to be in control, since control is what we lacked as children.
---sometimes we need a lot of space. Pressuring us to have sex will only increase our tension.

6. We often experience physical discomforts, pains, and disorders that are related to our emotions.

7. We often appear to be extremely strong while we are falling apart inside.

8. There is nothing wrong with us as survivors -- something wrong was DONE to us.

9. Sometimes others get impatient with us for not "getting past it" sooner. Remember, we are feeling overwhelmed, and what we need is your patience and support. Right now, it is very important for us to concentrate on the past. We are trying to reorganize our whole outlook on the world; this won't happen overnight.

10. Your support is extremely important to us.

Remember; we have been trained to hold things in. We have been trained NOT to tell about the abuse. We did not tell sooner for a variety of reasons: we were fearful about how you would react, what might happen, etc. We have been threatened verbally and/or nonverbally to keep us quiet, and we live with that fear.

11. Feeling sorry for us does not really help because we add your pain to our own.

12. There are many different kinds of people who are offenders. It does not matter that they are charming or attractive or wealthy. Anybody -- from any social class or ethnic background, with any level of education-- may be an offender. Sexual abuse is repetitive, so be aware of offenders with whom you have contact. Do not let them continue the cycle of abuse with the next generation of children.

13. We might not want or be able to talk with you about our therapy.

14. We are afraid we might push you away with all our emotional reactions. You can help by: listening, reassuring us that you are not leaving, not pressuring us, touching (WITH PERMISSION) in a nonsexual way.

15. Our therapy does not break up relationships - it sometimes causes them to change as we change. Therapy often brings to

the surface, issues that were already present.

16. Grieving is a part of our healing process as we say goodbye to parts of ourselves.

Testimonials from

Healing from Abuse*

*www.healingfromabuse.webs.com

Ranked #94 out of hundreds of websites in Website Reviews in the Health Category.

"So good to hear your story…what hit home for me was that you described much of my life through my teens – until I left for college…"

Kate: "I was sexually abused by three cousins and it began when I was six years old. It lasted until I was 10, when they all got 'real' girlfriends. At 19, I ran away from home to get married to the first guy I dated. Nine abusive years later, I divorced him, and moved in with a man who never cheated on me, but was even more aggressively abusive. In 2004, I tried to take my own life; was two days in intensive care, and seven days in a mental ward. Through all this, God was with me, and in 2008 I finally summoned the strength to get out of the horrible torment I was in (I went back to this man after the hospital stay). In the process, God put a godly man in my life that's patiently helped me heal ALL the wounds inflicted by others. We've been married for two yrs now and finally, all the past is behind me. I take no medication and have no 'flashbacks'. I put all my trust in God, and he has rewarded me with a wonderful husband and a better life than I could have imagined."

Rebecca

Evangelist, full-time ministry

"Found your site. Thank you for helping survivors. I am a survivor of childhood sexual abuse. Even 42 years later I am still trying to deal with what happened to me. I recently told a friend of my family's what happened and she seemed to feel like it was my fault for not telling my mother or anyone when it was actually happening to me. I did try, but often victims are terrified to tell and this was my case. So thank you for this site. I don't feel alone."

Jennifer

'1 learned a lot on this site how to get things out from inside of me. Writing things out is very freeing. "   Strong Tower

---

"Thank you, I've been on this page, your topic information searching is the best I have ever found."

Anonymous

Transfer Egypt - great website

forget me not - - I Think this site is a good website for information

bracknelllamps - great resource

lexiyoga - Great site. I like what you have to offer. Good stuff:)"

"Hi Barbara,

Excellent site and good for you to do this! Awesome! Thank you for caring for yourself and other victims of abuse. Thank you for your understanding and concern and effort. Always,

Lisa"

"I have difficulty with my emotions after talking about my abuse. I have huge anxieties. Getting out of bed to go to work or any other activity is difficult. And I have never told my story to anyone while I have been sober. I'm 46 years old, and never had a real relationship in my life. My goal is to get people to trust me, but I never really trust anyone else. I did in my teens and it bit me in the ***. "Don't get so defensive" I have heard a lot in my life. And the big one: "just get over it". Do survivors usually go thru a lot of jobs in their life? I have. And when you have anger, is it common to be self-loathing?"

Dorothy

When people
walk away from you …
Let them go…
Your destiny is never
tied to anyone who
Leaves you, and it
doesn't mean they are
bad people.
It just means
that their part in
your story is over.

Unknown

Biography

Barbara has lived her life with the terrible consequences of sexual abuse overshadowing her as she played as a child into her adult years as a wife and a mother. She did not know what she experienced as a child was abuse until she was 45 years old when her husband purchased a book to help them answer questions and anguish that they were experiencing together. She found out that of the 35 symptoms of abuse, she had 34, and had learned to deal with the aftereffects of feeling unloved, worthless, and suicidal as best she could. It took a toll on her marriage and family until she sought help with the Community Mental Health of West Michigan.

There, she learned about DBT (Dialectical Behavioral Therapy) where she practiced managing her emotions within a small group of people who were battling with the same kinds of things. Belonging to a group such as that validated her and made her feel that she wasn't alone in what she felt; that it was real and it wasn't her imagination.

Barbara spent six long years in therapy telling her story to a wonderful therapist, Amy, who understood her and believed her. She then learned how to get past the perceptions that kept her from leading a normal, healthy life, such as feeling the need to be invisible or perfect, phobias, depression, suicidal ideation, trust issues, boundary issues, feelings of shame and guilt, low self-esteem, abandonment issues, blocking out childhood years, dissociation, and feeling different from everyone else. She spent days in bed crying and unable to function. She also lost her successful business which she had built herself from the ground up. Everything had turned to shambles. Barbara learned that everything she believed was a lie, and sought hard to find the Truth of her existence.

She did find that Truth, that God loved her and created her just as she was, and He wasn't to blame for the abuse she experienced. She found forgiveness for her abusers and that though she hated them for damaging her life so intensely, she loved them very much. They were the people she grew up and nothing could change that. She found understanding and love from her husband and also her kids, who were in their teens.

Barbara developed a passion for helping others who were dealing with abuse. She began a website to do just that, and to this day, as grown to over 27,000 visitors and continues to be an informative tool for many people around the world. She has helped literally thousands of people with the insight she has gained through her own experiences.

Another passion was the love of writing. She began writing as a high school girl, penning her thoughts and feelings as she struggled to survive emotionally. Now she felt that she must tell her story of healing that people need to hear so desperately and began to write several books, a lifelong dream of hers. The first book she has published as an e-book on Kindle, is through Amazon and is about the steps she learned to use to heal. They brought her from a life of depression and suicidal thoughts to one of vibrancy and laughter, making "real" friendships with people she comes in contact with. She hopes others will find healing as they read her book. It is also being published in book form and can be found on www.Amazon.com. The title of it is "10 Healing Steps Out of the Pain of Abuse".

She has been given the opportunity to share around the world, putting many books in the hands of people from Africa and Portugal, The Russian Federation, The United Kingdom, Germany, Chile, The United States, and many more. She plans to publish additional books on abuse.

Barbara is now in college at Ferris State University, working toward her Masters in Social Work. She plans to practice therapy and counseling when she graduates, continue sharing her story through speaking, and continue to help all that come to her to find some relief of the abuse they are experiencing.

There is hope and healing to those who have been abused.

A sexual abuse survivor, Barbara is the founder of Healing from Abuse, (www.healingfromabuse.webs.com), an online ministry that seeks to bring hope and healing to those who have been abused. The website has over 28,000 readers from all over the world in just four short years since its inception. She longs to see that each person who has been abused to find freedom, peace and purpose through their suffering through her website, books, and experiences.

Barbara and her husband, Dale, live with their dog, Lacey, and their bird, Tweeter, near a resort village near Lake Michigan. She has three grown children and a son-in-law who live close by: Tasha and Will, Natalie, and Dale II, all of whom she adores spending time.

When she's not with her family, her hobbies include flower gardening, interior design, riding horses, writing, and remodeling their 19$^{\text{th-}}$ century country farmhouse into a cozy, comfortable home.

Recommended Books

* Secret Survivors, Uncovering the Aftereffects of Incest in Women
   This book contains a comprehensive list of symptoms of abuse.
   by E. Sue Blume

* Lord, Heal My Hurts
   by Kay Arthur

* When Rabbit Howls
   by Truddi Chase

* Repressed Memories
   by Renee Fredrickson, PH.D

* The Stranger in the Mirror. Dissociation - The Hidden Epidemic
   by Marlene Steinberg

* Beginning to Heal
   by Ellen Bass and Laura Davis

* Multiple Personality Disorder from the Inside Out
    by Barry Cohen

* The Dissociative Identity Disorder Sourcebook
    by Deborah Bray Haddock

* A Mind of My Own
    by Chris Costner Sizemore, author of Eve
* Amongst Ourselves
    by Tracy Alderman and Karen Marshall

* Magic Daughter
    by Jane Phillips

* Betrayal of Innocence
    by Dr. Susan Forward and Craig Buck

* Incest and Sexuality
    by Wendy Maltz

* Caring for Sexually Abused Children
    by Dr. R. Timothy Kearney

* The Myth of Sanity
    by Martha Stout

* Not Child's Play,
    by Risa Shaw

* Ghosts in the Bedroom
    by Ken Graber

* I Hate You, Don't Leave Me, Understanding the Borderline Personality
  by Jerold J. Kreisman

* Allies in Healing
  by Laura Davis

* First Person Plural
  by Cameron West

* The Courage to Heal
  by Laura Davis

Helpful Websites

Online Support Groups

http://www.isurvive.org/
This is the first support group I joined.
Wonderful site for community and finding
out that you are not alone. Very welcoming.

MERCY MINISTRIES - *Free nationwide and*
international therapy
http://www.mercyministries.org/splash.htm

FIND A THERAPIST NEAR YOU

NetworkTherapy.com
A Mental Health Network
http://www.networktherapy.com/directory/find_thera
pist.asp?gclid=CliPyKjS56cCFU9pKgodEkU6bg

FreedomCounseling.com
Wichita, KS

Fountain Hill Center for Counseling,
Grand Rapids, MI
www.fountainhillcounseling.com

Spiritual Resources

FIND PEACE WITH GOD
http://www.proverbs31.org/doyouknowJesus/doYouKnowJesus.php

The Pocket Testament League
FREE GOSPEL OF JOHN FOR YOUR SPIRITUAL GROWTH
http://www.ptl.org/

"Lord, Heal My Hurts"
Book by Kay Arthur
http://http://store.precept.org/p-529-lord-heal-my-hurts.aspx
Kay Arthur was one of the first authors who really helped me to deal with my pain before I knew I had been sexually abused. It is where my own healing journey began back in 2003. I highly recommend this book. Another good book of Kay's is "Lord, Is It Warfare?" *You'll love them!*

God So Loved You
http://peacewithgod.jesus.net/god-so-loved-the-world/

The Harbor House of Hart
www.theharborhouseofhart.org
Their purpose is to serve and set free young women at risk,
Building up and changing their lives for the Glory of God.

Speaking Engagements

Barbara travels to speak to groups who are interested in hearing her story of success in overcoming the pain of incest and mental illness. It is a story that will encourage you on your own journey, that healing is possible after all. Email her today to speak to your group. barbarakompik@hotmail.com

"Barb was fantastic! We have done many of these trainings and never had officers give a standing ovation at the end of the consumer's

presentation...something akin to a spiritual

experience! Let's keep in touch."

Michigan Commission on Law Enforcement,

about 40 in attendance.

Barbara's Life Verse:

"...Fear not: for I have redeemed you; I have called you by name, (Barbara); you are mine. When you pass through the waters, I will be with you; and through the rivers, they will not overflow you: when you walk through the fire, you shall not be burned; neither shall the flame kindle up. For I am the Lord your God..."

~ Isaiah 43: 1b-3a KJV (paraphrased)

Eventually you will come to understand that love heals everything, and love is all there is.
~ Gary Zukav

"God is love"

I John 4:16 KJV

Disclaimer:

Barbara Kompik *is NOT a mental health
professional at this time. However, she is working
diligently toward her Masters in Social Work at
Ferris State University, Big Rapids, Michigan with
plans to go into Therapy and Teaching.*

Contact Barbara

Barbara would love to hear from you!

Contact her at:
barbarakompik@hotmail.com

Or

Oceana Dr., Hart, MI 49420

Facebook: Barbara kompik

Facebook Group: 12 healing steps out of the pain of abuse

Facebook Page: healing from abuse

www.HealingfromAbuse.webs.com

and let her know how you are doing on your healing journey.

To order additional books, please visit www.Amazon.com.

You may be interested in her upcoming books:

Healing from Abuse: Finding My Voices
Little Boy Blue: Prose & Poetry from
Survivors of Abuse
The Melding
Letters to My Therapist

My children and I: Tasha & Will, Dale II, Natalie

My husband, Dale and I

Go in peace

God be with you

Amen and Amen

Made in the USA
Middletown, DE
08 November 2019